PICTURE LIBRARY

MONKEYS
—AND APES—

PICTURE LIBRARY
MONKEYS
—AND APES—

N.S. Barrett

Franklin Watts

London   New York   Sydney   Toronto

© 1988 Franklin Watts Ltd

First published in Great Britain
    1988 by
Franklin Watts Ltd
12a Golden Square
London W1R 4BA

First published in the USA by
Franklin Watts Inc
387 Park Avenue South
New York
N.Y. 10016

First published in Australia by
Franklin Watts
14 Mars Road
Lane Cove
2066 NSW

UK ISBN: 0 86313 638 9
US ISBN: 0-531-10529-6
Library of Congress Catalog Card
Number 87-50849

Printed in Italy

Designed by
Barrett & Willard

Photographs by
Survival Anglia
Pat Morris
ZEFA
Bruce Coleman/Helmut
    Albrecht (front cover)

Illustrations by
Rhoda & Robert Burns

Technical Consultant
Michael Chinery

Contents

Introduction

Monkeys and apes are humans' closest relatives in the animal world. After human beings, they are among the most intelligent animals.

Humans, apes, monkeys and some other relatives called prosimians make up the primates. The primates are the highest group, or order, of the animal kingdom. They vary in size from the fearsome-looking gorilla to the tiny mouse lemur.

△ An angry mountain gorilla. Many people think of gorillas as fierce animals, but they are mostly gentle creatures with few enemies. Like other apes, they live on the ground as well as in trees. They eat only fruit and leaves.

Most monkeys and apes live in
tropical and subtropical regions of
the world. Their natural homes are
the forests and grassy areas of South
and Central America, Africa and
southern Asia.

One of the chief differences
between apes and monkeys is that
apes, like human beings, have no
tails.

△ A red colobus
monkey from the
tropical forests of
Africa. Monkeys are
very agile and use their
tails for balance to help
them swing through the
trees.

7

Looking at monkeys and apes

Where they live

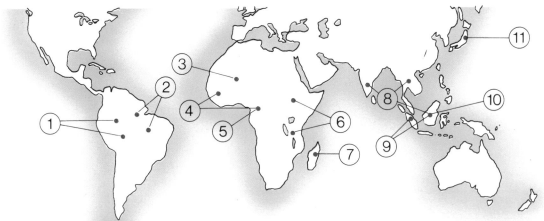

1 Pygmy marmosets, tamarins, night monkeys, uakaris.
2 Howler monkeys, sakis, capuchins.

3 & 6 Baboons, vervets.
4 Chimpanzees. **5** Gorillas.
4–6 Bushbabies. **7** Lemurs, indris, aye-aye.

8 Langurs, macaques.
9 Orang-utan, gibbons.
10 Proboscis monkey.
11 Japanese macaque.

Making faces

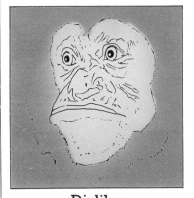

Dislike

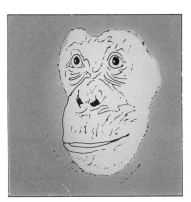

Thoughtful

Sad

Monkeys and apes communicate with each other by sounds and gestures. Like human beings, they show their feelings by the expressions on their faces. Chimpanzees have the most expressive faces. Not all their expressions are like those of humans. You can tell their feelings more from their mouth and lips than from their eyes.

Hands for gripping

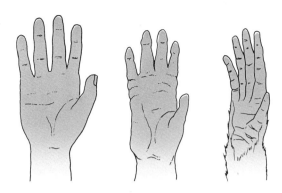

Human   **Chimpanzee**   **Gibbon**

Chimpanzees' hands are very much like human hands, with a thumb that can be used for gripping objects. The long, slender hands of the gibbon are used for gripping branches as it swings at speed through the trees.

Biggest and smallest

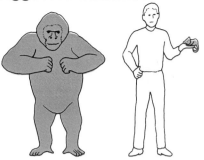

The gorilla stands almost as high as a tall man. The mouse lemur fits easily into a human hand.

Bones and skeletons

The bone structure of human beings and apes is very similar. Although monkeys and apes can stand upright, human beings are the only primates who walk upright all the time.

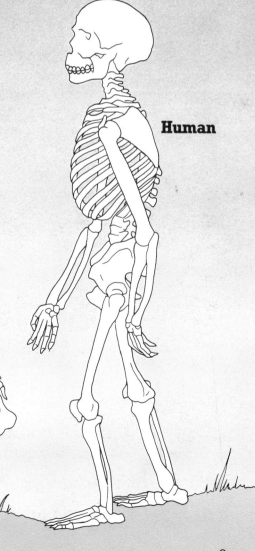

Human

Chimpanzee

Kinds of monkeys

There are nearly 150 kinds, or species, of monkeys. Scientists divide them into two major groups. The New World monkeys live in Central and South America, the Old World monkeys in Africa and Asia.

All New World monkeys live in trees. Some Old World monkeys, such as the many kinds of baboons, live on the ground.

△ A spider monkey swings through the trees, using its tail as a fifth limb. Such a tail is called "prehensile" because it can be used for grasping. Only New World monkeys have prehensile tails. Spider monkeys are so-called because of their spiderlike appearance.

Most kinds of New World monkeys have flat noses with the nostrils at the sides. The nostrils of Old World monkeys are close together. Of the two major groups, Old World monkeys are usually larger, and the male may be twice as big as its mate.

The prosimians include several kinds of lemurs and some small nocturnal, or night-living, creatures of Africa and Asia.

▽ The indri is the largest of the prosimians, about 80 cm (31 in) long. Indris belong to one of the lemur families, which live on Madagascar, a large island off the east coast of Africa. Unlike many other lemurs, they are "diurnal" animals, active in the daytime.

▷ A group of Japanese macaques bathe in a warm pool even though there is snow on the ground. They live in the high forests of Japan, farther north than any other monkey, and enjoy the warmth provided by hot springs. Apart from human beings, they are one of the few primates who can withstand freezing temperatures and snowy conditions. They are often known as snow monkeys.

They are the largest of the macaques. Most macaques live in southern and eastern Asia. They have a long muzzle and feed on leaves and fruits as well as insects and worms and other small animals such as mice, lizards and even crabs.

Heads . . .

△ A black-faced guenon (left), from eastern Africa, and a young baboon (right).

◁ The emperor tamarin, a tiny "flat-nosed" New World monkey.

▽ A red uakari (left) and a white-faced saki monkey (right), both from South America.

△ Top: A stump-tailed macaque (right) of southern Asia and a pair of female black lemurs (left).

△ Center: A bushbaby (left), a squirrel monkey (middle) and an aye-aye (right).

◁ The golden-headed lion tamarin is a tiny New World monkey that lives in Brazil.

. . . and tails

△ A ring-tailed lemur (top left) and a female black lemur (above).

◁ A lion-tailed macaque standing on a branch. Seen in silhouette like this, its shape resembles that of a lion.

▽ Gray langurs (bottom left) and a pig-tailed macaque (below).

Kinds of apes

There are four main kinds of apes. Gorillas, orangutans and chimpanzees are known as "great apes." Gibbons, the fourth kind, are known as "lesser apes."

Apes live in tropical Africa and Asia. They have hairy bodies with no tails, and their arms are longer than their legs. Like monkeys, great apes normally walk on all fours, but in a more upright position.

△ A male gorilla stands guard as a youngster crosses a road in the forest. A great ape supports the front part of its body on its knuckles.

Gorillas live mainly on the ground in groups of from 2 to 20, usually led by an adult male. Older males are called "silverbacks" because of the patch of white hair that develops on their back.

Scientists have carried out studies on the intelligence of the great apes, especially chimpanzees. They have taught chimpanzees and gorillas to communicate in sign language.

In some sign-language experiments, chimpanzees have learned to use grammar and to make up sentences. This sort of ability shows far more intelligence than, for example, a parrot's imitations.

▽ A half-grown male chimpanzee. Chimpanzees live in the tropical forests and wooded grasslands of western Africa. They dwell in trees as well as on the ground. Their main diet is fruit, but they also eat insects and small birds and mammals.

△ Two siamang gibbons (right), one with her baby, and a young orangutan (top left). Gibbons have especially long arms and are very agile. The slow-moving orangs are the largest of the tree-dwelling primates. Both gibbons and orangs live in Southeast Asia.

◁ Old male orangs, especially those in captivity, develop huge swollen flaps around their faces, giving them a fantastic appearance.

How they live

All monkeys and apes except the orangutan live in social groups. Some, such as gibbons and marmosets, live in family groups of mother, father and young, like human beings.

In the most common type of group, several males, females and young live together. Some types of monkeys, such as hamadryas baboons, live in "one-male" groups. In these, an adult male is the leader.

△ A group of yellow baboons, with males, females and young. They live on the edge of forests and spend much of the day looking for food. At night they climb up in the trees for safety.

Groups of monkeys that live on the ground need strong leaders so that they can protect themselves against their enemies. Hyenas, jackals and the big cats such as leopards and lions are monkeys' chief enemies.

Monkeys and apes spend much of their time foraging for food. Most kinds of monkeys will eat almost anything they can get, from plants, nuts, and insects to frogs, birds and other small animals.

△ A group of rhesus monkeys gathers for feeding in northern India. These macaques have survived the destruction of many of their natural homes in forest and woodland by living in towns and villages. They often raid gardens and rubbish dumps or are fed by the people.

△ Monkeys and apes love all kinds of fruits. A baboon (top left) tucks in with relish to a kigalia, a tropical fruit. A young orangutan (above) enjoys as many small bananas as it can carry.

◁ The douroucouli, or night monkey, is the only New World monkey that is active at night. Also called owl monkeys, they live in South America in small family groups, and spend most of the night searching for food.

▷ Monkeys and apes communicate with each other by gestures and sounds. The gibbon has a very large throat sac and can sing and hoot loudly, warning other gibbons not to intrude on its territory.

▽ Adult baboons enjoy grooming each other to clean their fur. They spend several hours a day in this activity.

Growing up

Most kinds of monkeys and apes give birth to one baby at a time. At first, the young are almost completely helpless and cling to the mother's breast. Soon they are able to ride on the mother's back.

The young stay within the social group until they become adults. This might be as long as 14 years in the case of gorillas, for example.

▽ A black-faced vervet monkey grooms her youngster. The young of vervet monkeys, a common species in Africa, are fussed over by all the female monkeys in the group.

▷ A baby spider monkey clings to its mother's back as she leaps through the trees. She supports the baby with her tail.

▽ A toque macaque baby clings to its mother's underside as she runs along the ground. The baby curls its tail around its mother's for extra grip.

◁ A young baboon plays in the forest, swinging from a thin branch just off the ground.

▷ Young gorillas watch and imitate a game warden in an African national park.

▽ Baboon youngsters enjoy a friendly game under the watchful eye of a mother. The young are very playful and are full of tricks.

The story of monkeys and apes

Ancestors

Monkeys and apes come from the same ancestors as human beings. By studying ancient animal remains called "fossils," scientists have built up a picture of how the various primates have developed. The picture, however, is like a jigsaw with many pieces missing. But we think that our early ancestors probably looked like tree-shrews.

△ Millions of years ago, our ancestors probably looked something like this tree-shrew.

Development of primates

The first primates lived on the earth billions of years ago. These shrewlike creatures lived in trees. Like squirrels, they climbed by digging their claws into the bark. Over millions of years, they developed longer fingers and toes that could grasp branches. Their eyes became larger and more forward-looking.

This gave them the ability to judge distances better and to move more easily through the trees.

△ One of the most curious-looking primates is the proboscis monkey, from the jungles of Borneo, in the East Indies. Yet the long bulbous nose of the adult male gives it an almost human appearance.

Primates of today

The primates developed in several distinct ways. Our distant cousins the prosimians come from an early stage of evolution. They have remained small and look more like their ancestors than the other primates.

The ancestors of the New World monkeys were cut off from the rest of the world several million years ago, so they developed in different ways from the Old World monkeys. The apes developed much later.

△ A baboon with a youngster on her back and a radio collar around her neck. The radio helps scientists monitor the baboon's movements as part of a study program.

Classification

The animal kingdom is divided into a number of groups called "classes." The primates are one of the groups that belong to the class called "Mammalia," or mammals, which suckle their young. The primates are divided up into 13 families, which include the Hominidae, or human beings. The great apes make up the family Pongidae. Other families include the Old World monkeys, the New World monkeys, and the gibbons. The marmosets and tamarins make up another family.

The other seven families are prosimians, or primitive primates. Prosimians include the lemurs, bushbabies, lorises, pottos and the aye-aye, which has a family to itself.

Survival

Man has destroyed the habitats, or living areas, of many animals to build cities or to carry on such activities as farming and mining. All of the apes and many kinds of monkeys are in danger of dying out.

Game reserves and national parks have been set up in many countries to preserve wild animals. Even so, monkeys and apes are still hunted to sell as pets or for use in research. In some places, people kill monkeys for food. Monkey meat is eaten throughout West Africa and in the Amazon region of Brazil. Monkey brains are eaten in China. It is difficult to guard the areas where monkeys live because they are mostly in poor countries. But money collected around the world is used to help save our cousins from extinction.

Facts and records

△ The mandrill, from the rain forests of Africa, is the largest monkey.

Largest

The largest primate is the mountain gorilla, with an average weight of about 195 kg (430 lb), although it stands only about 1.75 m (5 ft 9 in), the height of an average man.

The largest monkey is the

△ The mouse lemur.

mandrill, with a weight of up to about 45 kg (100 lb). The adult male mandrill has the most brightly colored face of all mammals.

Smallest

The smallest primate is believed to be the mouse lemur of Madagascar, which weighs on average only about 60 gm (2 oz). The world's smallest monkey is the pygmy marmoset of South America, which weighs little more than the mouse lemur. Both creatures measure about 15 cm (6 in), not counting the tail, which is a little longer than the body.

△ The pygmy marmoset.

The hamadryas baboon

The only primate apart from man that lives on more than one continent is the hamadryas baboon. It is found in Africa and Asia.

Glossary

Diurnal
Active in the daytime.

Extinction
The dying out of a species.

Fossils
Animal remains such as bones or an impression preserved in rock.

Game reserve
An area where the wildlife is protected.

Great apes
The gorillas, orang-utans and chimpanzees.

Habitat
The type of area where an animal lives, such as a rain forest or grassland.

Mammal
An animal with body hair and mammary glands, or breasts, with which the mother suckles her babies.

National park
A designated area in a country where animals and their natural habitats are protected.

New World monkeys
The monkeys of the Americas.

Nocturnal
Active at night.

Old World monkeys
The monkeys of Asia and Africa.

One-male group
A group of monkeys dominated by a single adult male.

Order
A subdivision of the animal kingdom. The primates are an order of mammals.

Prehensile tail
A tail used for gripping.

Primates
The order of mammals which includes man, apes and monkeys.

Prosimians
The more primitive primates such as lemurs and bushbabies.

Sac
A pouch.

Species
A particular kind of animal. The members of a species are alike and can breed with each other. For example, the siamang and the lar gibbon are two different species of gibbon.

Index